# Main Street-Colorado.com
# Business Training Series

ⱭⱭⱭ

# MANUFACTURING BODY LOTIONS
## &
# BODY BUTTERS

ⱭⱭⱭ

*Professional Instruction By*
# Timothy M. Braun
## &
# Anita M. Braun

© 2018 Timothy M. Braun & Anita M. Braun

www.MainStreet-Colorado.com

**Sangre de Cristo Publishing, Inc.**
Cripple Creek, Colorado

*No part of this book may be reproduced, transmitted in any way, stored in a retrieval system, or otherwise without prior permission of the copyright holder except as provided by USA copyright laws.*

Copyright © 2018 Timothy M. Braun & Anita M. Braun
All rights reserved.

Printed in the United States of America.

*Cover design by Timothy M. Braun*

Published by Sangre de Cristo Publishing, Inc.,
P.O. Box 1003,
Cripple Creek, CO. 80813

**Kindle digital edition available at www.amazon.com**

# MANUFACTURING BODY LOTIONS

Don't be nervous about the word "manufacture", it is synonymous with the word "make," as in 'we make our own products.'

Definition of Manufacturing from WEBSTER:

1: something made from raw materials by hand or by machinery

2: the process of making wares by hand or by machinery especially when carried on systematically with division of labor

3: the act or process of producing something

Mid 16th century (denoting something made by hand): from French (re-formed by association with Latin

manu factum 'made by hand'), from Italian manifattura.

Manufacturing your own products is very easy and much more profitable than buying/selling products from a Multi-Level Marketing company or from a wholesaler! Most retailers in a brick and mortar store make approximately 50% on their sales. I am going to show you throughout this series how you can make upwards of 70-90% on your sales.

Would you like a GREAT home business manufacturing your own products that are needed and wanted? Do you have a retail business and would like to <u>add custom-made</u> manufactured products to your line that your customers would love and need?

Now's the time to start your own profitable business! You don't have to be a brain surgeon to start a business. It's not the easiest, but it's not hard… it just takes a lot of work and a commitment to be in business for yourself.

It's fun, especially after you've done all the hard work getting started, and when everything comes together and you start selling or obtain some major orders. Some will probably be large; large enough to pay for all your investment and give you a nice profit.

**Those of you who are selling for an MLM** (Multi Level Marketing) company; are you really making any $$ with Avon, Mary Kay, Amway, Tupperware, Legal Shield, Young Living, DoTerra or any other MLM? Are you working hard, making sales, but don't seem to see many profits because of all the fees and hidden costs associated with your business? It has been shown that up to 99% of those selling in an MLM don't really make any REAL $$. Some MLM's advertise their "agents/ associates/partners/sales people" make 30,40 & even 50%. BUNK!! After you subtract all the fees, the cost of mandatory meetings, the flyers/receipt books/marketing materials, the samples, the stock and all the other items you are required to purchase (and many times can't sell), many people end up making no $$ at all or end up in the negative. They tell you it's an investment! Again, BUNK!! That's a business? NO, it's not even close, and many are continually sucked into the promises of big $$ and their own business!

So, I researched who is really making all the money. I found it's the manufacturers, the people at the top. Check it out for yourself.

Would you like to be at the top? Would you like to make $$ and REALLY control your own destiny?


I am going to show you later on in this book how you can do all this for yourself, and you can start out small and still make a great profit! We did it and so can you! We will start you out with lotions and body butters, as they always sell the best. We'll get into all the other items in other books, as you need to learn the basics first.

Whether you are a stay-at-home mom or dad, retired, handicapped or whatever, you can create a business that makes real $$ -- right from your home and give you the extra $$ you want or need!

When you manufacture/make your own Bath & Body & Home products you can make upwards of 80%+ profits on your products, or upwards of 600-800% ROI (Return on investment) by starting your own line of Bath & Body & Home products. They are ultra easy to produce and we are going to show you everything, step by step!  You can literally have fun; even make it a family business, and possibly turn your products into a GREAT business!  There are no quotas or goals to meet.  Work and learn at your own pace.  There are no sales meetings you have to attend, no sales tiers to work towards.  Your rewards are the goals you set and reach for yourself.  You are your own boss.

Why sell someone else's products when you can sell your own? You can wholesale, or retail for the greater profit.  Advertise your products as ***__Made In America!__***  Most national brands can't say or do that as most are manufactured overseas.  Many customers will pay a premium for anything made in America, and many others will pay a premium for locally made products.

Build your business by selling to school or non-profit fundraisers; sell on Etsy, at fairs, craft shows, churches, your own website, social media, etc.  Your world is unlimited to where you can sell retail, or wholesale your products to local businesses.  The sky is the limit.

We started manufacturing our own products over six years ago and have learned much in the industry, while selling hundreds of thousand of dollars in products. It was hard starting out, as we had to purchase large quantities of everything to get decent pricing in the Bath & Body & Home business in order to make a decent profit wholesaling. We had to purchase thousands of dollars of bottles and pumps and caps and fragrances and lotion bases. It was extremely expensive, but there was nowhere we could get just what we wanted starting out with decent pricing. We had over $10,000 invested just in fragrances and essential oils. This is one of the areas where we help you out getting started. We purchase in bulk and pass those savings on to you, no matter how much you purchase, because we want you to succeed. Want 2 or 3 of a certain color of bottles or caps? No problem. Want a small amount of a certain fragrance or essential oil? No problem. We are here to help you along your path to success. The items we will be teaching you to manufacture, we have sold thousands of them, all manufactured by us.

If you never take that first step, nothing ever happens. Every time you resist something new, you hinder yourself from achieving anything. Fear actually stops you from going forward. We understand this. This is an opportunity, a chance to take an opportunity, to connect with someone who has done it and use our experience to take yourself to the next level. We do this by letting you get started with a minimal expense, and if you like it and are making $$, you can go to the next level. Wherever you are today, just start! Take charge of your future!!

# FAQ's

1. Do I need any prior knowledge to get started?

A. No, we teach you everything, from the very basics to the technical.

2. Is there a membership or initiation fee?

A: No, the only costs are the supplies you will need to start to manufacture your products. All businesses have expenses associated with them. You will need to purchase the supplies necessary to manufacture the products.

3. What supplies will I need?

A: We suggest you start manufacturing just a few products first, get used to the process and then add products as you feel comfortable, obtain orders or want to add to your line. We are starting you out with lotions and body butters.

4. Where do I learn how to manufacture and obtain training?

A. We have videos planned for the future, so until we have our videos finished, you will be able to simply follow the instructions we give you in this book for each item you manufacture. We provide all the documentation you need for you to refer to.

5. Do I need a business or a sales tax license?

A. In order for us to not charge sales tax (where we have to) you will need a business license if your city/county/state requires one to do business. You will also need a sales tax license if your city/county/state requires one. In Colorado, you will probably need both. Although **you** won't charge sales tax on wholesale sales, all sales will usually still have to be reported if you are a business.

6. Can I get started without a business license or sales tax certificate?

A. Yes, you can order your supplies to get started, but we may have to charge sales tax in Colorado. Wherever you are, you are always better off with a business license. When you start selling and wholesaling, you will need a business license.

7. What other Bath & Body & Home products do you teach?

A. Are you ready? Face Creams, Face Masks, Body Mists, Body Sprays, Foaming Hand Soaps, Shaving Butters, Perfumes (Oil Based and Alcohol Based), Foot Balms, Moisturizing Lotion Bars, Nail & Cuticle Conditioner, Ultimate Body & Skin Therapy, Hand Balm, Lip Balms, Room & Linen Sprays, All-natural base Glycerin Shea Butter Bar Soaps, All-natural base Glycerin Cocoa Butter Bar Soaps, All-natural base Glycerin Goat Milk Bar Soaps, All-natural base Glycerin Aloe Vera Bar Soaps, Bath Bombs, Fragranced Bath Salts, Body Wash, Fragranced Body Salt Scrubs, Shampoos, Conditioners, Men's Aftershave Gel, Beard Oil, Men's Moisturizer, Men's Body Wash, Men's Body Spray, Men's Spray Cologne, Men's Hand & Body Lotion, Men's Shaving Butter, Candles, Massage Candles... and more! We don't have all the books for them yet, so email us, visit us or give us a call if you have a priority item you would like to manufacture!

We are open from 10-5 Mountain time zone or email us anytime at MainStreetColorado@gmail.com. You can also visit us at The Hitchin' Post, 333 E. Bennett Ave., in Cripple Creek, CO.

## **Here are some actual costs and profits you should see by manufacturing your own Bath & Body & Home products.**

Q. ---I'd like to see an example of making over 70% profits on my first order under $75! (Total Cost: $71.18; Total sales from those costs: $254.85; Total profit from those sales: $183.74)

A. All right, here goes: A gallon of one of our finest lotions will cost you $48.95. That will make (16) - 8oz lotions; 15 will cost: ((128 oz ) / 16) x 15 = $45.89). 3 bottles of different fragrances will be $2.90 each or $8.70. Usage will be 83% of the 3 bottles or $7.22 for 15 - 8 oz lotions. 15 clear pumps will be 58.5¢ ea or $8.78. (15) 8 oz Boston bottles will be 49.6¢ ea or $7.29. A sheet of 15 glossy labels is $2.00. Add them all up and it comes to $71.18.

You shouldn't sell this 8 oz lotion for less than $16.99 (you can sell it for whatever you want). $71.18 total cost divided by (15) - 8oz lotions, comes to your cost of $4.745/ea or $12.245 profit ea. $4.745 divided by the selling price of $16.99 equals your cost of 27.9% of the selling price or 72.1% profit. All of this is at the start-up discount. As you grow and order more quantities, your discount becomes greater and thus your profit becomes greater.

Let's look at the 4 oz lotions. A gallon of our finest lotion, again, will cost you $48.95. If we were to make (15)-4 oz lotions that is 46.8% of the gallon. That cost would be $22.91. 2 bottles of different fragrances will be $2.90 each or $5.80, and that will give you 30 ml of fragrance. We will only need 18.75 ml at the most, which is 62.5% of $5.80 or $3.63. 15 metal dispensing caps will be 63¢ ea or $9.45. (15) 4 oz Boston bottles will be 46¢ ea or $6.90. A sheet of 15 glossy labels is

$2.00. Add them all up and it comes to $44.89. Your cost is $2.992 / bottle.

I sell these 4 oz lotions for 9.99 (you can sell it for whatever you want). Your cost is 29.9% of sales & gives you a 70.1% profit margin.

Q. ---I'd like to see another example of a different item making over 70% on my first order under $100!

A. Okay...A gallon of our Premium body butter will cost you $46.95. That will make (16) - 8oz body butters; 15 will cost ((128 oz) / 16) x 15 = $44.015). 3 bottles of different fragrances will be $2.90 each or $8.70. Usage will be 83.3% of the 3 bottles or $7.25 for 15 - 8 oz body butters. (15) 8 oz Double Wall jars will be $1.30 ea or $19.50. A sheet of 15 glossy labels is $2.00. Add them all up and it comes to $72.76.

You shouldn't sell this 8 oz body butter for less than $16.99 (but you can sell it for whatever you want). $72.76 total cost divided by (15) - 8oz body butter comes to your cost of $4.85/ea or $12.14 profit ea. $4.85 divided by the selling price of $16.99 equals your cost of 28.5% of the selling price or 71.5% profit. All of this is at the start-up discount. As you grow and order more quantities, your discount becomes greater and thus your profit becomes greater.

Q. Any more?

A. **Want an example of 80% profit margin?** Let's do roll-on perfume. This is one of our better profit items and they sell very well. A glass bottle with roller and cap will cost you $1.49/ea. 15 of them will be 22.35. A bottle of 4 oz body oil will be $5.99 and that will give you enough for 15 roll-ons. You use 2 ml of fragrance or essential oil in each roll-on. 2 bottles of half ounce different fragrances will be $2.90 each or $5.80, and that will give you fragrance for 15 roll-ons. A sheet of glossy labels is $2.00. Add them all up and it comes to $36.14.

I sell this 10 ml roll-on perfume for $12.99 (you can sell it for whatever you want). $39.07 total cost divided by (15) - 10 ml roll-on perfumes comes to your cost of $2.41/ea or $10.58 profit ea. $2.41 divided by the selling price of $12.99 equals your cost of 18.5% of the selling price or 81.5% profit. All of this is at the start-up discount. If you add the velour perfume bag & plastic bag/label, (see it at MainStreet-Colorado.com) there will be a small additional cost. As you grow and order more quantities, your discount becomes greater and thus your profit becomes greater.

Here is a chart with some of the numbers I just quoted you plus a few more.

| | Bottle | Jar | Cost Base | Label | Cap | Pump | Frag | ml-frag | Sugg Sell @ | Cost | Profit | profit % |
|---|---|---|---|---|---|---|---|---|---|---|---|---|
| **Masage Oil-$29.95/Gal** | | | | | | | | | | | | |
| Masage Oil-8 oz | $0.49 | | | | $0.63 | | | | $12.99 | $3.12 | $9.87 | 75.95% |
| Masage Oil-4 oz | $0.46 | | | | $0.63 | | | | $8.99 | $2.16 | $6.83 | 76.00% |
| Masage Oil-2 oz | $0.41 | | | | $0.63 | | | | $5.99 | $1.64 | $4.35 | 72.62% |
| **Lotion-GMHS-$48.95/Gal** | | | | | | | | | | | | |
| 8 oz | $0.49 | | $3.059 | $0.133 | | $0.585 | $0.465 | 2.500 | $16.99 | $4.73 | $12.26 | 72.15% |
| 4 oz | $0.46 | | $1.529 | $0.133 | $0.630 | | $0.232 | 1.250 | $9.99 | $2.98 | $7.01 | 70.13% |
| 2 oz | $0.41 | | $0.764 | $0.133 | $0.630 | | $0.116 | 0.625 | $6.99 | $2.05 | $4.94 | 70.63% |
| **Lotion-Satin & Silk / Aloe & Shea -- $54.95/Gal** | | | | | | | | | | | | |
| 8 oz | $0.49 | | $3.434 | $0.133 | | $0.585 | $0.465 | 2.500 | $16.99 | $5.11 | $11.88 | 69.94% |
| 4 oz | $0.46 | | $1.717 | $0.133 | $0.630 | | $0.232 | 1.250 | $9.99 | $3.17 | $6.82 | 68.25% |
| 2 oz | $0.41 | | $0.858 | $0.133 | $0.630 | | $0.116 | 0.625 | $6.99 | $2.15 | $4.84 | 69.28% |
| **Lotion-Basic-$29.95/Gal** | | | | | | | | | | | | |
| 8 oz | $0.49 | | $1.871 | $0.133 | | $0.585 | $0.465 | 2.500 | $9.99 | $3.54 | $6.45 | 64.52% |
| 4 oz | $0.46 | | $0.935 | $0.133 | $0.630 | | $0.232 | 1.250 | $6.99 | $2.39 | $4.60 | 65.81% |
| 2 oz | $0.41 | | $0.467 | $0.133 | $0.630 | | $0.116 | 0.625 | $4.99 | $1.76 | $3.23 | 64.81% |
| **Body Butter- Premium / Avocado Body Butter $46.95/Gal** | | | | | | | | | | | | |
| 8 oz | | $1.30 | $2.928 | $0.166 | | | $0.465 | 2.500 | $16.99 | $4.86 | $12.13 | 71.40% |
| 4 oz | | $0.90 | $1.464 | $0.166 | | | $0.232 | 1.250 | $9.99 | $2.76 | $7.23 | 72.35% |
| 2 oz | | $0.70 | $0.732 | $0.166 | | | $0.116 | 0.625 | $6.99 | $1.71 | $5.28 | 75.48% |
| **Roll-On Perfume** | | | | | | | | | | | | |
| 12 ml | $1.49 | | $0.392 | $0.133 | | | $0.390 | 2.000 | $12.99 | $2.41 | $10.59 | 81.49% |
| **Shaving Butter- Men - $54.95** | | | | | | | | | | | | |
| 8 oz | | $1.27 | $3.434 | $0.166 | | | $0.465 | 2.500 | $16.99 | $5.34 | $11.66 | 68.60% |
| 4 oz | | $0.99 | $1.717 | $0.166 | | | $0.232 | 1.250 | $9.99 | $3.11 | $6.89 | 68.92% |
| 2 oz | | $0.89 | $0.858 | $0.166 | | | $0.116 | 0.625 | $6.99 | $2.03 | $4.96 | 70.96% |

**Getting Started- Supplies**

Manufacturing body lotions and body butters are some of the easiest products to manufacture after you have everything in place. There are many decisions you must make first. This may seem daunting at first, but it's really not. After you make the following decisions, everything is easy!

1. What do I need to purchase before I start any manufacturing?

    a) One time purchases supplies

There are a few things you must purchase locally before you get started.

- A digital scale. Purchase one that has ounces, grams and pounds. This is an item you will use for practically all your manufacturing. If you ever get into large-scale manufacturing you will probably have to purchase one that is certified.

- Zip Lock baggies. Get the sandwich size, quart size (optional), and a gallon size. Don't cheap out here and get a bargain brand. They leak at the seal edges and you will be disappointed. Get the double zip lock type.

- Keep a supply of paper towels available at hand.

- You will need a bottle of alcohol for cleaning the pipettes you use for measuring fragrances/essential oils.

- Purchase a good set of scissors for trimming the stems of pumps.

b) Manufacturing supplies

The types of manufacturing supplies to stock is what you believe will sell the best.

- Do I want to offer coloring in my lotions?

I have never had anyone ask for coloring. You can offer it if you wish, but I believe it is an unnecessary expense and time mixing.

- What types of bottles do I want to offer?

We offer both the Boston type bottle and the tall, narrow type, Cosmo bottle. The Cosmo bottle seems to sell the best in our store.

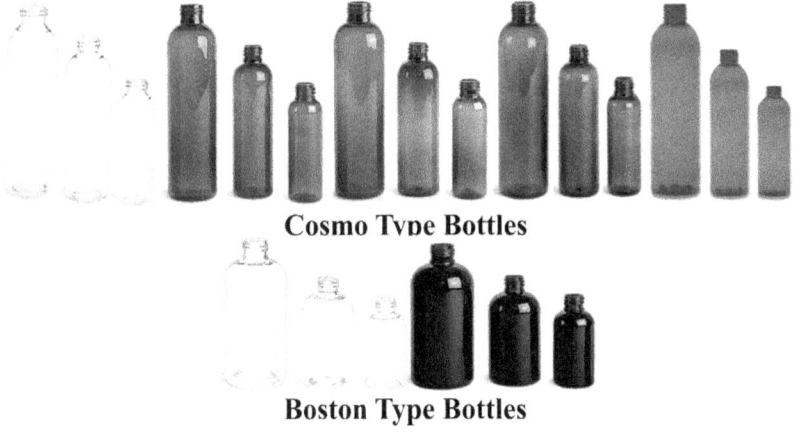

**Cosmo Type Bottles**

**Boston Type Bottles**

- What sizes of lotions (bottles) do I want to offer?

We offer our customers the 2, 4, & 8 ounce bottles. I started to discontinue the 2 oz bottles at one time, and then discovered that women like the 2 oz to keep in their purse. I also have the one-ounce bottles, but I recommend staying away from them to start out with, as they don't sell very well in lotions.

- What colors of bottles to I want to offer?

We offer six different colors of bottles to our customers for custom lotions. Clear, Cobalt blue, emerald green, red, black and amber. Our best sellers are clear and Cobalt blue.

- What types of pumps will I offer for 8 oz bottles?

The pump we use for the Boston bottles is the clear pump. For all the Cosmo bottles, we use the black pump. The pumps are for 8 oz bottles only. The openings of the 8 oz bottles (24/410) are larger than the openings of the 4 & 2 oz (20/410).

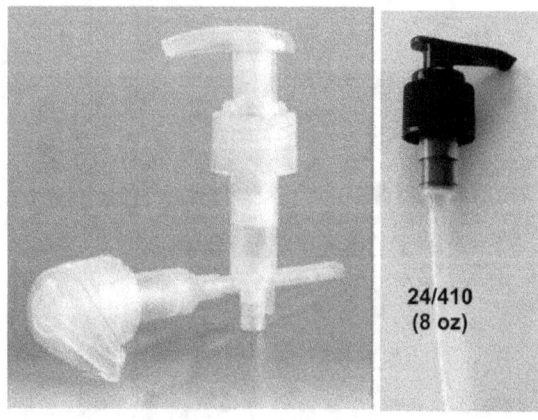

24/410
(8 oz)

- What types of dispensing caps can I offer for the 2 & 4 oz bottles?

The dispensing caps we use for all the bottles are the gold and silver types. They are a little more expensive than using a black or white cap, but it makes your brand look a lot more high-end. The dispensing caps come in two sizes. The 8 oz bottles are (24/410) are the 4 & 2 oz (20/410).

- What types of jars are best for my Body Butters?

Most women will prefer a white double wall jar. These are a little more expensive than a single wall, but it makes your products look very professional. You can also always use a colored jar. I use a cobalt blue jar for the men's products. I have also used the clear jars seen below.

- What is the name of my line going to be?

Here is where you need to put a lot of thought into your brand name. Some people like using their name in the brand, some put the name of their city or locality in the name. I always recommend not doing that. If you ever go to sell your brand, someone or a corporation may not want to purchase your business simply because of the name. Think of a great name that has universal appeal!

- What is the label design?

Again, put a lot of time and effort into this one. Once it's designed, show it around and ask your friends and relatives what they think of it. Just small changes can make a big difference.

If you have a design in mind, but don't know how to do it, go to Fiverr.com. There are hundreds of people there that will design your label for a few bucks, usually $5-$10. It may be a little more for ornate designs, but I have always had good luck there. In designing your label, remember you have to leave room for the ingredients, your contact information (Business name & address is advised), weight in ounces and milliliters, usage instructions, any warning statements and your URL if you have a website. You can also put the suggested retail price on the label if you want and also the "Made in America"..

Here is an example of my 8 oz Goat Milk, Honey & Shea label, Satin & Silk and Cocoa Butter.

It took a long time to arrive at this label; I went thru many different types before settling on this one. I will let you use my different labels, but you must change the name of the business on it. Let me know if you want to see my other ones.

## How much am I going to charge?

First, consider your time and costs so you can come up with what it costs you. Beyond that, this is purely a decision on your part. I always believe being somewhere in the middle to upper end is the wisest choice. There is an adage that you can always come down on your price with specials and sales, but it's really hard to go up!

One of the first things you want to consider is where you want to position yourself in the industry. What do I mean by positioning yourself? It means at what level of sophistication would you like to see your products. Do you want to be on the level of a cheap Walmart bulk type product or one of the more sophisticated products that cost more? Do you want to sell your 8 oz lotion for $9.99, $16.99, $19.99 or $25.99? What type of customer are you selling to and whom do you want to attract? In addition, if you start your products out at $19.99 or more, it leaves you room to have a special or a sale price, which is lower, but still makes a nice profit.

There are literally hundreds of cheap knock-off brands and you will get lost in the crowd if that is your customer. Position yourself as a higher-end product and you will attract that type of customer for even more of your products. . If they believe they are getting value for their money, they will continue to purchase.

**Decide what bases you are going to use.**

You can go to www.MainStreet-Colorado.com and sign up with us for manufacturing to get the best pricing on our lotion and body butter bases. We give you a password to access that section of our online store. There are many to choose from or you can shop elsewhere.

**The lotion bases we sell are:**

**Goat Milk, Honey & Shea Butter** – (97% Naturally Derived Ingredients) Water, Glyceryl Stearate, Isopropyl Myristate, Caprylic/ Capric Glyceride, Stearic Acid, Stearyl Alcohol, Cetearyl Alcohol, Ceteareth 20, Soybean Oil, Shea Butter, Dimethicone, Sunflower Oil, Aloe Barbadensis, Goat Milk Extract, Hydroxypropyl rimonium Honey, Benzophenone, Methylparaben, Propylparabaen, DMDM Hydantoin, Triethanolamine Disodium EDTA.

**Satin & Silk -** (our thickest lotion) (97.63% Naturally Derived Ingredients) - Ingredients: Water, Glycerol Sterarate, Isopropyl Myristate, Cetearyl Alcohol, Ceteareth 20, Caprylic/Capric Glycerides, Dimethicone, Stearyl Alcohol, Soybean Oil, Shea Butter, Sunflower Oil, Hydrolyzed Silk, Aloe Barbadensis, Disodium EDTA, Diazolidinyl Urea, Benzophenone 4, Iodopropynyl Butylcarbamate, Triethanolamine.

**Cocoa Butter** - Ingredients: Aqua, Theobroma Cacao, Cocos Nucifera, Vitis Vinifera, Emulsifying Wax NF (Vegetable Based), Palm Stearic Acid, Vegetable Glycerin USP, Aloe Barbadensis, Oenothera Biennis, Tocopherol (Vitamin E), Sodium Hydroxymethylglycinate, Phenoxyethanol (Mild Preservative Blend) Has a Natural Chocolate Aroma.

**Aloe & Shea Butter -** (98% Naturally Derived Ingredients) Water, Glyceryl Stearate, Isopropyl Myristate, Caprylic/Capric

Triglycerides, Stearic Acid, Cetearyl Alcohol, Ceteareth 20, Shea Butter, Dimethicone, Sunflower Oil, Aloe Vera, Disodium Benzophenone-4, Iodopropynyl Butylcarbamate, DMDM Hydantoin

**The body butter bases we sell are:**

**Premium Body Butter**– Ingredients: Deionized Water, Octyl Palmitate, Grapeseed Oil, jojoba oil, hemp oil, Cetearyl Alcohol, teareth-30, Ceteth-10, Cetyl Alcohol, Stearyl Alcohol, Chamomile, Boswellia Serrata, Tocopherol, Borage Seed Oil, Carbopol, Triethanolamine, Propylene Glycol, Diazolidinyl Urea, Methylparaben, Propyl-paraben.

**Avocado Body Butter** – Ingredients: Deionized Water, Avocado Oil, Glycerin, Stearic Acid, Cetyl Alcohol, Dimethicone, Glyceryl Stearate, PEG-100 Stearate, Oryza Sativa (Rice) Bran Extract, Rosmarinus Officinalis (Rosemary) Leaf Extract, Helianthus Anuus (Sunflower) Extract, Tocopherols, Panthenol, Allantoin, Triethanolamine, Phenoxyethanol, Hexylene Glycol, Caprylyl Glycol, Ethylhexylglycerin.

**Whipped Body Frosting** - Ingredients: Deionized Water, Cetearyl Alcohol and Cetearth-10, Theobroma cacao (Cocoa) Seed Butter*, Glyceryl Monostearate, Isopropyl Palmitate, Butyrospermum parkii (Shea Butter) Fruit*, Aloe barbadensis (Aloe Vera) Leaf Juice, Triethanolamine, Tetrasodium EDTA, Methyl Paraben, Propyl Paraben.

So now we have all that out of the way and you have decided on which lotion and/or body butter bases you are going to use, we can talk about actually making them!

## Making your products.

--Using your scale, measure out 8.1-8.2 oz's of your chosen base into a Zip Lock sandwich bag. Determine whether you are going to be using a dispensing cap or a pump for your lotions. The 8 oz bottles will actually take 8.1 to 8.5 oz's of lotion. The pumps take up a bit of space in the bottle so you can always go with a straight 8 oz's. If using a dispensing cap, and you are using a clear bottle, it may look like you are not full. In this case I usually give about 8.2-8.3 oz. You will usually have a small amount of lotion left in the bag as a film, so that extra tenth of an ounce we initially started out with is for that. In addition, if you are going to give exactly 8 oz's in the colored bottles, I always give at least an extra tenth of an ounce. That is up to you! The body butters in jars can be exact amounts, but consider giving a little extra in each.

If you are making 2-5 (8 oz) lotions or body butters at one time, use the gallon bag. You will have to multiply the weights you want to use and multiply the milliliters (ml) of fragrance and additives below.


--Now you are ready to add your fragrance or essential oil. I use the following guidelines for adding fragrances. I always ask the person I am making the lotion for if they would like it scented light, medium or heavy. Most will say medium or heavy.

I have never seen a fragrance where you can't add at least 1.5% to lotions to be skin safe. The following amounts are all approximately 1-1.2%.

8oz- Heavy scent --2.5 milliliters (ml)

    --Medium scent --1.25 ml

--Light scent -- .75 ml

4oz--Heavy scent --1.25 milliliters (ml)

--Medium scent --.75 ml

--Light scent -- .5 ml

2oz--Heavy scent --.625 milliliters (ml)

--Medium scent --.3 ml

--Light scent -- .2 ml

Since essential oils are stronger than fragrances, I use about three-quarters of the fragrance strength. You should always test your fragrances and essential oils and develop your own chart of what to use.


Now you can always add any special body oils that your customer my want added if you decide to offer it. Our lotion bases will easily take 1-3 milliliters of any of the following body oils:

Olive Oil

Argon Oil

Coconut Oil (use MCT)

Avocado Oil

Shea Butter Liquid

Aloe Vera

Soy Bean Oil

Sunflower Oil

Marula Oil

Safflower Oil

Sesame Seed Oil

Hemp Oil

Clear Jojoba Oil

Golden Jojoba Oil

Evening Primrose Oil

Seal the bag and hold it like in the next photo to mix the contents thoroughly. This is to make sure the seal doesn't open on you! Make sure you mix in the corners of the bag. After a couple minutes carefully move some of the lotion to the upper part of the bag to make sure you have all the fragrance/essential oil mixed in.

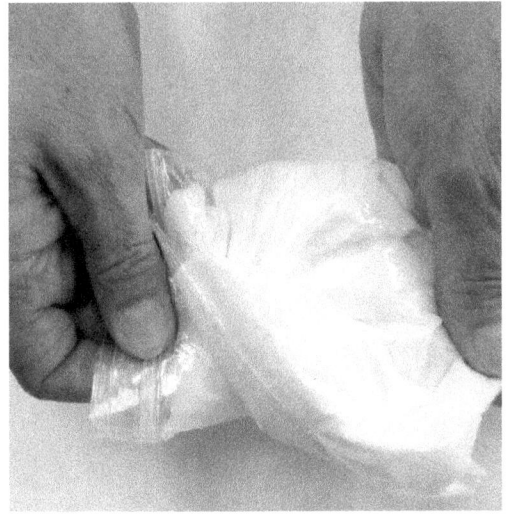

(Hint: If your customer can watch you make their lotion, they are usually amazed. I always open the bag after mixing and ask them if the fragrance is strong enough if they chose the light or medium scent.)

(Hint: If you would like to see how long it actually takes to thoroughly mix a bag of lotion, add in a couple drops of food coloring or lotion coloring to see how long it takes for everything to come to an even color. That is how long you should take to evenly disseminate the fragrance/essential oils.)

--Now, you ask, how do we get the lotion into the bottle? Easy! Trim a small piece off the corner of the baggie (see picture) and squeeze the lotion into the bottle. Hold the top of the bag as shown as you don't want it coming open. The heavier the lotion (the Satin & Silk is thick) the larger the cut should be. As you get to the top of the bottle, you will have to tap the contents down several times. (See the following photos.)

1. – Lay bag on table or flat surface and push
the lotion away from one of the lower corners.

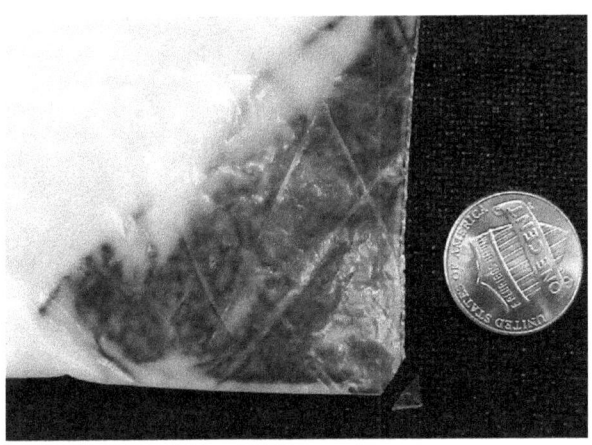

2. – Carefully snip a SMALL part of the corner. Make
sure it is very small. You can always snip more if needed.

3. – Carefully squeeze the contents of the bag into the bottle. This is just like putting icing on a cake! Take your time. As the bottle fills, you will have to tap the bottle on the table to settle the contents down into the bottle. Keep doing this when the lotion gets too high.

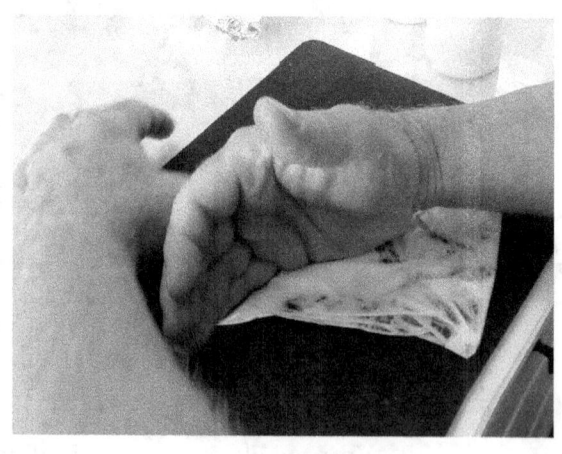

4. – When the bag is almost empty, flatten bag on the table and with the edge of your hand, push the balance of the lotion towards the cut corner and you will get the last of the lotion. The best way to get all the lotion out is to use a flat edge item like a pencil and push all the excess lotion to the edge.


-- Next, if you are using a pump, you will have to trim the stem. Hold the pump up to the bottle at the height it would be as if in the bottle and trim it just above the bottom of the bottle, as the bottoms are concave. (see photo)

Cut the stem at an angle.

**Cut at Angle
Here**

--Apply your label(s).

Pipettes will come in a 1 ml and 3 ml size. The 1 ml pipette is marked at quarter ml's and the 3 ml is marked for half ml's. (See photo)

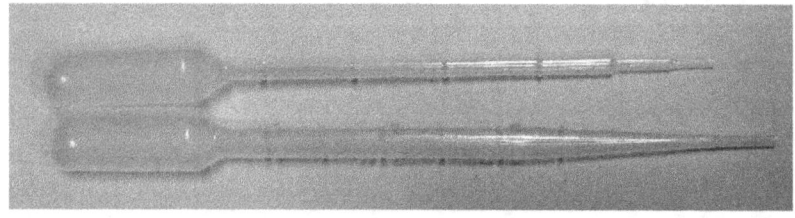

NOTE: If you are making these products for sale, good manufacturing practices recommend a clean workspace, you wear a hairnet, gloves and a mask. We also recommend a clean apron.

## SEALS

If you are making your lotions for a store or wholesale, I recommend using a bottle seal for the bottles with a cap. This will show the customer the product hasn't been tampered with and will keep others from taking a "sample". The seal will adhere to the bottle when you place the cap on tight. They are self-sealing. You need to make sure the top of the bottle is clean for it to seal. I suggest wiping it with alcohol to let the seal adhere tightly. Place the seal in the cap and screw on tightly. The seals come in different sizes, so specify the small (20/410) or the large (24/410).

- Sangre de Cristo Publishing, Inc is not responsible for the products you create from our supplies, recipes, or instructions. You alone are responsible for product and recipe testing to ensure compatibility and safety.

- While we work to ensure that product information is correct, we strongly recommend you do not take medical advice from anyone except your doctor or assume that a product will work the same for you or others. Every consumer is different, circumstances vary and interpretations of results vary.

- Sangre de Cristo Publishing, Inc. assumes no liability for inaccuracies or misstatements about products in this book.

- Over pours or under pours may affect the percentages of profits.

# Appendix A
## Recommended Printers, Inks & Labels

I have no financial interest in the printers or the inks I am going to talk to you about. I only recommend them as they are the ones I use.

**Let's talk about labels for a moment.** This is probably what is going to attract your customer more than anything else. It's basic marketing. If you make a quality label that attracts the eye, you will be more successful than using a plain label that doesn't attract anything. I can't overstress the need for a quality label. It will also help you position your products at a higher level. So spend the time necessary to develop a quality label. Again, put a lot of time and effort into this one. Once it's designed, show it around and ask your friends and relatives what they think of it. Just small changes can make a big difference.

If you have a design in mind, but don't know how to do it, go to Fiverr.com. There are hundreds of people there that will design your label for a few bucks, usually $5-$10. It may be a little more for ornate designs, but I have always had good luck there. You don't have to be an expert at computer design. I have used www.fiverr.com many times to get something done that I didn't know how to do. It is only $5 and some of the designers on there are really good. If you find one who really knows their stuff, stick with him/her and throw a little extra to them once in awhile and they will do wonders for you. I had a logo that was just two colors and basically just a line art. I asked one designer to color it and make it more three-dimensional. He did a great job and I gave him an extra $10. He was happy and I got something I would have had to pay hundreds for if I hired someone at a design company.

CHARTER MEMBER

The left one is what I gave him to work with (2-color); the right one is what I got for just $5 (Full Color)!! It was a great deal!

I had the following logo done for a cookie store. I told them what I wanted and she came up with the following. She charged me $20. I thought it was a real bargain.

Always make sure you have the rights to any photo or logo or design you intend to use. There are many copyrighted label designs out there for sale, so make sure you get the rights to use any design forever.

You will need labels for each item, usually in at least three sizes (2oz, 4oz, 8oz). We will print them for you if you wish, or supply the sheets of labels for you to print your own. Your labels are an important part of your products. Take time to design a great label. No one will be attracted to a product with a drab or dull label. It has to make your products stand out.

I suggest always using a gloss or a weatherproof label. It makes the colors you use brighter, makes them "pop". It also holds up better in a bathroom environment where many products will be used.

You may ask how do you do that. One of the easiest and cheapest ways is to get the right printer.   Now, you can have the labels printed by a commercial printer, but starting out, that can get very expensive. With just lotions, if you offer three different types of lotions with three different sizes, that's nine different labels you will have to have printed and most of time, at a minimum, you'll have to have hundreds of each printed.

I suggest to everyone just starting out, invest in an Epson color printer. Why Epson? There are two different types of inks used in today's printers, dye and pigment. Epson is the only printer that uses pigmented inks. This is what you want as the ink sits on top of the label/paper, makes the image "pop", not into the label/paper as a dye ink does. Also, the ink is "archival", it's supposed to last almost a hundred years without fading, etc.

The best place to purchase your Epson printer is at Epson.com. They have sales all the time and you can get some great deals. In addition, you can get 2-year insurance very cheap. They also have the good ole standby, the Stylus C88 for $119.99. If you are just going to do labels, this will do perfectly well and **www.injetcarts.us** has the refillable cartridges for them. (See below) If you are going to ever print T-shirts, I would recommend getting a printer that will take 11x17 paper as you can use basically using the same inks.

You can purchase ink for your printer where it costs you practically NOTHING! You know those $10, $15, $20 ink cartridges? Never again!! Go to **www.Inkjetcarts.US** and find a list of Epson printers they support. Purchase the refillable cartridges and the corresponding inks and you will be able to print for years for almost nothing!

*Epson WORKFORCE WF-7610 #252XL Refillable Resettable*
*Ink Cartridges  $19.95 a set at:*
*https://store.inkjetcarts.us/wf7610-usa-c1560.aspx*

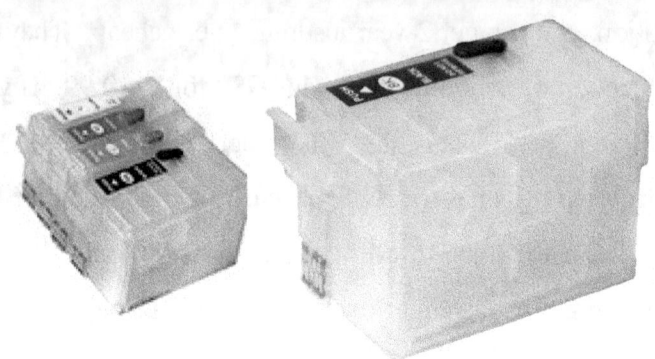

*InkJetCarts Epson Durabrite Ultra Compatible DuraMaxx*
*Pigment Refill Inks-$40.00/set*
https://store.inkjetcarts.us/inkjetcarts-epson-durabrite-ultra-
compatible-duramaxx-pigment-refill-inks-p6507.aspx

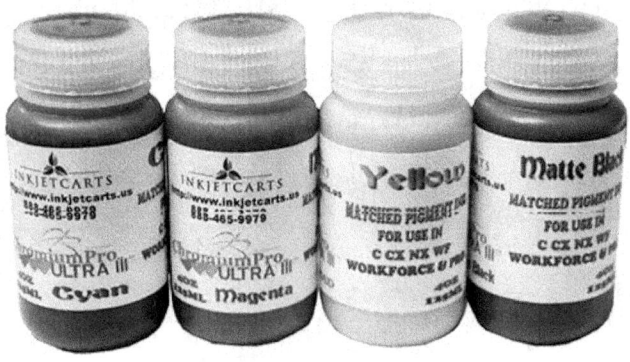

Some will ask, why not a color laser printer?  Well, I have tried
and sampled many color laser printers.  I don't like them
because you really can't get a true red out of them, and a good
color red attracts the eye.  They all seemed very dull or had an
orange tint to them.  Maybe if you purchased a $1000- $2000

printer, you might get the quality you need, but I tried many of the office versions that were in the $200-$500 range and they didn't live up to my expectations. The Epson inkjet printers will cost approximately $100-200.

To help you out, I'll even print your labels for you, but you have to obtain your designs first. I'll give you the sizes I need to print at for the labels you choose. I charge an extra $2.00/ page for printing plus a one-time layout/setup.

## Appendix B

### Manufacturing Insurance

If you ever attend fairs or other places to sell your Bath & Body items, most of the venues will require insurance. If you ever obtain a large wholesale customer and they require insurance, or you just want insurance, here is where you can get it very cheaply. They specialize in small business policies. I use them. You can see the coverage limits below and it is usually sufficient for any customer. They will NOT cover candles.

# Annual Policy
## Policies include the following:

- Instant Coverage
- Immediate Proof of Insurance
- 24/7 Access to Policy
- A+ Rated Insurance Carrier
- $1M Coverage Limit for $285
- $2M Coverage Limit for $385
- Product Liability Included

*$285 Starting at/ per year*

Go to: https://www.handmadeinsurance.com/default.aspx